231.6
P18G
a

I0640943

BT
160
.P2
1904

GOD'S WHITE THRONE

A DEFENSE OF
Divine Wisdom and Goodness in the Dark
Things of the World and Life

BY

THE REV. BYRON PALMER, A. M., D. D.

*" And I saw a great white throne, and
Him that sat on it."*—REV. xx, 11

NINTH THOUSAND

CINCINNATI
PRESS OF JENNINGS AND GRAHAM
1904

COPYRIGHT, 1904, BY
BYRON PALMER.

Dedication

*I rejoice to dedicate this book to her, the
companion of my life, who, through the
years of my suffering and invalidism,
has been unfailing in her Christian
faith and fortitude, and by her
cheerfulness, courage, and devotion has made life sweeter,
hope brighter, and given to
suffering a compensation.*

THE AUTHOR.

000386

000356

PREFACE.

Several years ago, in reading the life of Charles Kingsley, I came upon these lines which he had written to a friend:—

"I am writing nothing now; but taking breath and working in the parish—never better than I am at present; with many blessings, and, awful confession for mortal man, no sorrows! I sometimes think there must be terrible arrears of sorrow to be paid off by me—that I may be as other men are! God help me in that day!"

Again he wrote:—

"I am better off now than I have been for years! God be thanked, and God grant, too, that I may not require to be taken down by some terrible trouble. I often fancy I shall be. If I am, I shall deserve it as much as any man who ever lived. I say so now—justifying God beforehand lest I shall not have faith and patience enough to justify him when the punishment comes."

I was deeply impressed by the fears and finally the experiences of that good man. For the "terrible trouble" did come to him at last. I wondered whether I should have the patience to endure and faith enough in God not to doubt or despair in case the hand of affliction ever should be laid upon me as heavily as I saw it resting upon many whom I knew.

I was then in the vigor of perfect health joyfully anticipating many years of service in the work which I had just begun and loved so much.

I had seen what seemed to be strange workings of providence affecting the lives of others, and had tried to encourage hope and faith and cheer in those who were bowed with sorrow or baffled with unbelief.

But as I had had no experience in the things that troubled others, I felt that what I said and did to help them must have been to them only a professional echo and not a voice out of a life that was capable of real sympathy.

Before my own life of suffering in silence and seclusion began, the larger problems of darkness and disorder in the world, and in human life in general, were driven home to me by a conversation which I had with a noted infidel. He doubted the existence of a God who took any interest in human life, and denied that there was any goodness or wisdom in the order of the world. He declared that there was no good God, no moral government—all was heartless, blind, inexorable law; this and nothing more.

I felt that this was not true, but to myself I had to confess that sometimes it did look that way.

When at last came the ordeal of being

shut away from the world, and of leaving my life's work, and of being compelled to accept the life and the lot of a daily sufferer, my mind naturally turned to the problems which experience had made uppermost in my daily meditations. It became necessary for me to seek and find a satisfactory solution of, not only the problem of personal suffering, but of the larger problems of human life and destiny, of the apparent misadjustments in the world, of the seeming contradictions in the course of providence, of the absence of order in divine government, and the apparent defeat of righteousness and truth in the world.

In seeking for mental and spiritual peace in the midst of my own suffering and disappointment, I came to see as never before that the problem of personal experience did not stand alone, but was related to and was a part of every problem that involves the beneficence and wisdom of God's moral government in the world. My quest for peace of mind and heart therefore led me away from myself to the infinitely larger world without and to the relation which every soul sustains in the moral harmony of things in divine government. Not until then did I experience the faith in God and the patience to abide by his wisdom and goodness which gave me rest.

This book is therefore in a certain sense the author's experience in his effort to discover the ways and the will of God. But in a truer sense it is an effort to help all who are troubled with doubt and disbelief either from personal experience or from their observations in the dark hemisphere of the world's life. To all such the author extends his sympathy and the help which his experience may afford. Cordially,

BYRON PALMER.

ASHTABULA, OHIO, June, 1904.

CONTENTS

11

GOD'S WHITE THRONE.

CHAPTER I.

THE DARK HEMISPHERE.

WE live in a world of mystery. No matter which way we turn we are sure to meet with mystery before we have gone far. From the very nature of things deep shadows are cast all about us, and their darkness is not all dissolved by any view of life that we may take, however optimistic it may be, or by any conception of the world however comprehensive. The lives of some are cheered by greater joys and brighter hopes than others, scarcely a shadow falls upon them; while others dwell in the darkness with only an occasional star to bless them with its beam of holy light. It is therefore not taking a somber view of life and the world to recognize the dark things that are matters of common experience and observation with all men.

Consider the planet on which we live. Its surface is three-fourths a restless water waste, the grave already of millions of human beings. Of the remaining land surface a very large part is composed of dreary deserts, rock-ribbed mountain ranges and vast territories that are rendered uninhabitable by perpetual ice and snow. Devastating storms sweep away life and property, and drouths burn and blast the fruit of man's toil and sacrifice. The thin crust is shaken by subterranean explosions, and internal fires belch forth and burn and bury the helpless and the innocent. The history of the earth as recorded in the rocks reveals ages of agony and warfare among the extinct tribes of the lower animals, and natural history seems to indicate that the living species exist for the sole purpose of preying on one another.

and human society is so intimately organ-
ized that no man can live unto himself
alone.   Consciously or otherwise all men
reciprocally influence each other for good
or for evil.   But why for evil?   Why not
for good alone?   Why must an honest man
suffer because others by their dishonesty
have shaken the confidence of his fellow-
men?   Why must a worthy, aspiring youth
who happens to come from a disreputable
family or community be despised and dis-
criminated against as though no good thing
could come out of Nazareth?   Why should
the industrious and the frugal be burdened
by the necessities of the idle and the shift-
less?   Why must good government and
good society often be defeated and ever be
imperiled by the criminal, the pauper, and
the ignorant elements.   The law works for
good as well as evil, it is true; but why
must the helpless and the innocent suffer
under its operations?

Again, why should the truth be so ob-

scure? Why should truth and error be so
mixed that the world must ever be so mistaken as to their identity? Had the truth
been clearly defined, who can imagine what
a different course the history of the world
would have taken? Think of the wars and
persecutions and political and religious
strife and doctrinal controversies that have
arisen from error, ignorance, and intolerance! Think of the bloody work of the
guillotine, the stake, the gibbet, the scaf-
fold, the block, the dungeon, the rack, and
the hundred other torturous inventions of
fiendish ingenuity for extorting confession
and extinguishing the light of freedom and
truth, all because error and truth have been
so mixed that even the wise and conscien-
tious have been mistaken and thought they
were doing God's service in persecuting
the righteous! Among the lower animals
instinct is the sure guide, and for man's
animal life instinct and a small degree of
intelligence is sufficient; but for emanci-

pation of the mind and the upward flight of the soul's aspirations, for peace of heart and joy of hope, for sure knowledge of the truth and the right and an undisturbed confidence in a beneficent end for the world and human life, is it not strange that we have not more to help us and less to hinder? Yes, we have the Bible; but hundreds of sects and tens of thousands of teachers differ and divide on what the Bible means. Some say it is not inspired, some say it is inspired a little, some say it is inspired in places, while others say every word is inspired. Besides only a comparatively small part of the human family have ever seen the Bible as yet. There are other sacred books and other religions besides Christianity. Is the Bible the exclusive book of revelation? Why then does so large a part of the world yet sit in darkness, and why did so many centuries pass after the full revelation was given before its sacred pages were put in print and placed in the hands of the common people for their comfort and instruction?

Why did so many thousand years go by before the world's Redeemer came, and why was not some provision made for the immediate spread of his truth and grace among all nations? What do the dead and forgotten nations and literature and arts and civilizations and achievements of the early centuries of history signify for the present age? Why should we have to dig among the ruins of ancient cities and desecrate the tombs of the dead to find only a few chance fragments of the arts and culture and history and religious beliefs of antiquity? Is the human race a degenerate offspring from perfect parents, spotless from their Maker's hand, or is man the product of an almost endless process of evolution which began countless ages ago, of which firemist, protoplasm, mollusk, monkey, man, is an epitome? Is death the end? Where are the departed, and why may we not hold fellowship with them? Why should such a large per cent of the race die in infancy, and so few of those who survive ever rise above the plane of the animal life? Why should men and women having great promise of usefulness to the world so often die just when they are most needed and best prepared to do good, while others who are so wicked and worthless that it would have been better for the world had they never been born, are permitted to live on to curse the world rather than bless it? Why should parents be taken away leaving families of innocent orphans helpless and homeless? Why should so many who violate about every law of good health and pure morals still be healthy, prosperous, and popular, while others who practice plain living and high thinking, serving God and their fellow-men faithfully, become broken in health and spend the rest of their lives suffering in silence?

If there is light there is also darkness;

if truth, there is error usually mixed with it; if goodness, there is evil always near it, often looking even more attractive and better than the good; if songs of joy, they all have their notes of sadness. Alas, the list of evils that look like stains upon God's white throne is almost endless, and the darkness that occasions doubt deepens as one tries to enumerate and explain the mysteries that make up the dark hemisphere of our world's life.

But there is light along the horizon. If doubts arise, let us look to the light. If we despair, let us still keep our eyes fixed on the light. If hope should disappear, let us all the more resolutely keep our eyes on the golden promise of the morning. There is no other light, and the darkness is only a passing night. It is but temporal. The light is eternal. God is its source.

CHAPTER II.

Vanquished Faith.

FAITH in God is the normal attitude of the soul in the presence of all the unexplainable problems of human life. It seems to be a higher activity of the soul than reason, and is commissioned to lead in realms where reason loses its way. Where knowledge fails it is the function of faith to over-reach the narrower limits of the mind and lay firm hold upon the very substance of eternal realities. But naturally it is easier for us to believe what we can demonstrate, and when we can not demonstrate to doubt. Unfortunately we are so constituted.

But should there be any who do not doubt at times, the absence of doubt should not be considered a proof of the presence

of faith. In the absence of tests, faith may
be simply a passive mental process having
no moral content whatever. To be merely
an heir or recipient of what others have be-
lieved is not faith, for faith implies mental
and moral activity. He who has never suf-
fered in the dungeon of doubt may well
wonder whether he yet has had enough experience in the perplexing things of life
to put to the test what faith he may possess. Or he may question whether he
knows enough of the ways of God to have
any good ground for what he believes, or
be sure that he really believes much of anything.

But, supposing there are those whose
faith never fails them even in the severest
tests, there are many more who are equally
earnest, whose faith often gives way to
doubt and despair on account of the dark
things of the world and life. For the presence of so much physical and moral evil in
a world that is thought to be governed by

a beneficent God has caused more believers
to doubt, and has driven to despair more
seekers after truth than perhaps any other
fact of human experience. Nor is this sur-
prising. When we think of the uncertainty,
obscurity, physical evil, and moral disorder
that exist, the wonder is that there are not
even more who doubt whether there be any
good providence and moral order in the
world. Evil and error of every kind have
wrought such ruin and still run riot to such
a degree that it looks as though there were
an almost infinite demon at work in the
world, whose mischief makes about as much
misery as God's goodness gives of peace
and happiness.

In the presence of such mysteries both
reason and faith are often hurled back in
defeat, and doubt and despair triumph.

But there is an attribute in every man
that is sufficiently divine to cause him to
abhor the idea of an unrighteous, unholy,
and unwise God. He would rather have no

God at all than such an one. He would take refuge in atheism, rather than think that the infinite God is an evil-doer and the author of all the sufferings of the world, or in his helplessness is unable to prevent it.

It is therefore the creed of some and the thought of most people at times, that there is an evil one, some rival power who is the foe of God and the human race, who is the author of all this darkness and destruction. They will not have it that an infinitely good and wise God is responsible for so much confusion in his world. They therefore vindicate God and indict the devil, who it seems is almost equal to God and in much gets the best of him. If this could be done it would be an easy way for us to justify our impatience in times of trouble. We could then charge them up to the devil and be as vindictive as we wished. But it would not be so easy a matter to point out where infinite wisdom and goodness end, and where the evil work begins;

or what is good, and to whom and under what circumstances it is such. Any attempt to point out what is the work of divine goodness in this world, and what the mischief of a demon, would be preposterous.

But should we succeed in escaping the difficulty that perplexes us by attributing all that we call evil to a demon or any number of demons, instead of believing God is responsible for it, we are at once plunged into another that is equally perplexing to both our mental and moral natures. The universe would be divided against itself. God having abdicated his throne of absolute sovereignty, has divided his authority with an evil power whose energies are all devoted to confusion and destruction. But two rulers whose powers are in any proportion to the good and the evil that exist would be a fatal dualism. The attempt to explain existing evils in this way may indeed be worthy of an honest soul who cherishes and clings to his faith in God, but others would get no comfort from it. The rock that may be a firm foundation for his faith would wreck and ruin the faith of others. There is a more satisfactory course than this, as we shall see. God does not share his authority with another, and yet his throne is white.

There are many who do not pretend to understand or attempt an explanation of the dark and crushing facts of life. They do not doubt God's goodness, and yet they can not believe that all things work together for good to themselves or to others, even though they love God and try to do his will. They are not stoical or indifferent toward suffering. They feel deeply, and desire a smoother and firmer path for their feet. They wonder why there should be so little in life for them to enjoy, and so little for them to hope for in the future. To them the world is dark and life drags heavily. Bruised and brokenhearted, they bow

to the inevitable and spend their days in
sorrow. Like a bird with a broken wing,
they look upward, but can not fly. Hope
they have not. Faith has failed them,
but—God has not.

Others are so self-centered that all is
well while matters go well with them. They
can look upon the calamities that befall
others and maintain a well poised faith.
They may even reprove them for their lack
of faith and their inability to see some good
providence in their griefs and misfortunes.
But let broken health and blasted hopes
once come to them; let misfortune come
their way and deprive them of position or
property or reputation or loved ones; let
their lot be no more than falls to the aver-
age man; then they are of all men most
miserable. They will not be comforted.
Sympathy is only mockery. God will not
answer their prayers. He has abandoned
them entirely, or is dealing with them too
harshly. Their sufferings are unjust.

They lose faith in both man and God. The world is dreary, and life is to them not worth living. To work and to weep is their unhappy lot. They wish they never had been born. Out of the world: out of misery, they think. And yet this is the best conceivable world for them to live in. For not in the world, but within their own selves resides the power to make life sweeter than any song or richer than treasures of gold.

There are those too who have no faith in a supremely wise God, simply because they can not see wisdom and beneficence in the adjustments of the world. If there is a God and he governs in the affairs of men, they are opposed to his government. If they were to administer the governing forces of the world it would be managed better. Their self-esteem is sufficient to lead them to think that, had they been consulted about creation, they could have offered suggestions, which, had they been followed, would have brought into existence a better world than we have.

In all candor it will have to be admitted by every one that to the finite mind this world is an infinite enigma. But with equal candor it must also be admitted that inability to understand is no justification for doubt. Ought the child doubt his parents' love and wisdom because he can not understand why they require of him obedience and reverence, and deny him pleasures that are detrimental? Supposing the child to be entirely incapable of comprehending the wisdom and foresight of his parents, and what they believe to be for the highest good and happiness of their child, should the child still be commended for his disobedience and doubt, and the parents be censured for withholding from him the knowledge of things he can not comprehend?

We dwell in a world that is only as a pin-point on a mountain side when compared with God's vast universe, and our

3

life is but as a flash of candle-light to the eternally blazing sun, when compared with the numberless cycles of eternity throughout whose vastness the omniscient Mind moves with a perfect knowledge of the beginning and the end of all things. Should we then doubt God because we do not understand his motives and methods? Intolerable vanity and audacity might lead to this, but humility and modesty *never.*

Vanquished faith often takes the form of pessimism. Bad as the world is, it is continually growing worse. Evil and error are stronger and more prevalent than virtue and truth. Civilization is only barbarism made more cruel by refinement. The tendency of the human race is downward. Everything is undergoing a process of degeneration. There is no bow of promise arching the path of the world and no beneficent goal toward which the world is moving. Men, society, and nature alike are not to be trusted. Self-interest is the end sought, and the end justifies any successful means, even though truth and justice and virtue must be sacrificed in the effort. Christianity has departed from the life and teachings of its Founder, and the Churches which are supposed to exemplify Christ to the world are void of his life, his love, his truth, and his spirit of sacrifice. God is not in the world as a factor for good. But fortunately for the world there are comparatively few whose faithlessness takes this unhappy form, and as the world continues to grow better and brighter their number will ever grow less.

Dead faith is always more dangerous than honest doubt, for honest doubt has life and conscience and has its face toward the light, while dead faith gropes in the darkness, not even feeling after God and caring little for the light. Such a type of vanquished faith is the quite prevalent belief that God is so great and so far removed from men that it is unworthy of him to take them into account or feel in any sense obligated to them. Men are his creatures, and he has a right to do with them as he pleases. If he rules them with a rod of iron, what are they that they should protest or ask a reason why? It is for them to take what comes, and let things go as they may. From eternity the decree went forth fixing every man's fate, and nothing that he may do can better his condition or benefit the world. This is God's world absolutely. Good and evil, hope and despair, right and wrong, happiness and misery, life and death, are all equally his appointments, and they are unalterable. Stoically or sorrowfully we must take what comes, and be silent.

As an article of faith, as well as a principle for practical life, such a conception amounts to nothing short of harmful unbelief. It takes from God the attribute of condescending, fatherly love for his children, and it discourages the sense of responsibility, paralyzes good endeavor, does violence to the sense of justice in men, and quickens in them none of the finer feelings of spirituality. Instead of Sovereign, subject, and government, let us think of Father, family, and home. Such conceptions exalt God, elevate man to his proper relation with God, and give significance and inspiration to human life.

Closely related to this fatalistic form of vanquished faith is that which removes God entirely from the world. He transcends the world so far that he takes no thought for it, and feels no interest in his creatures. He created the world and established its goings according to fixed laws, and made it and all living things capable of self-perpetuation, and then ceased to be even an interested observer of the world's movements. According to this view the world is sufficient for all our wants, and we are left to make the best of it in satisfying them. There is no personal providence.

We are left to the cold mercies of heartless nature, which, though impartial, takes no thought for the peculiar needs of the individual. There is no revelation of God or inspiration from him except what nature affords, and that is sufficient. From the study of nature's laws and nature's wisdom we are to learn our duty and our destiny. There is no place for prayer. All answers to human supplications are but echoes of the soul's secret desires. There is no salvation except that which we achieve in co-operation with nature, no knowledge of God except what nature affords, and no hope of a future life except the soul's inextinguishable longings for immortality.

This type of disbelief is not occasioned by a serious contemplation of the dark things of the world and a failure to find some ground of consolation and hope, so much as by an unsound philosophy and an unethical conception of the nature of God.

As a system it hardly does credit to the mind, while the heart of every man protests against it and calls for clearer light when the soul is allowed to speak.

Honest doubt, for there is such, is always deserving of sympathy rather than censure. Nor is there anything gained in treating with contempt and severity the doubt that may be born of insincerity. To be fair and frank is the best course. Reasonableness and charity toward minds and hearts that are perplexed and depressed is the only method that is productive of good results. We shall try to show that while doubt may have its occasion, faith has firm ground, and for that reason is more justifiable than doubt, and in the rising soul will win at last.

But let the doubter bear in mind that faith is a law of social and commercial life, that society would not hold together without it, that commerce would at once be blocked should men cease to believe in each

CHAPTER III.

God Reigns.

That God is, that he is infinitely wise
and good, and that his wisdom and goodness are everywhere manifest, both in his
creation and in the interest that he takes in
the affairs of men, is the only conception
of him that fully satisfies the human mind
and heart. But that other things are set
forth as substitutes for God is very well
known.

We hear of the "laws of nature;" and,
from what is said of them and of what they
do, it would seem that they are about equal
to God and make a very good substitute
for him. But to make them so it is necessary to endow them with all the attributes
of the infinite God, whose place of authority in the universe they are supposed to

occupy. Their reign is universal and eternal. Their intelligence is so perfect that they work with definite design and development toward ends moral and spiritual that are far beyond the power of the human mind to comprehend or imagine. This wonderful system of laws is affected by no sickly sentiment toward the individual. It is in the interest of the highest good of the universe as a whole that they work. This is the beneficent end toward which through infinite ages they are progressing.

Sometimes the "forces of nature" are represented as sufficient to account for the world and its progress, and they, too, have all the attributes of an infinite Mind. They are eternal, and, far back in the morning of all existence, back so far that one's mind reels in its efforts to imagine, these mighty forces began the work of evolving this beautiful world of ours and the countless suns and systems that compose the stellar world, all from the lifeless fire-dust which then filled the boundless ocean of space. For numberless ages these wonderful forces have been faithfully working wisely and beneficently toward ends that would do credit to infinite Intelligence. All that these forces require is plenty of time. Give them infinite ages in which to work out their designs, and they are equal to any task.

But what do these terms "natural laws" and "natural forces" mean? A little thought-analysis will show that these laws and forces are not self-existing and self-acting and self-directing at all.

Laws never do anything, and natural laws are no exception. They tell us the way in which forces act, and the regularity of their procedure. Civil laws do nothing. It is the civil officer who acts, and the law is the course which he is to take as an officer, and the course which, as an officer, he is expected to cause all citizens to observe. Civil laws are therefore only the methods of civil and social order. The same is true of laws in nature. They are methods of order in nature, and define the course of acting, natural forces.

But what of natural forces? Are they not self-existing and self-acting? Or are they also blind, impersonal things without intelligence or wisdom or goodness? If the latter were true we should be no nearer the truth than we should be in attributing the world and its progress to simply natural laws. Natural forces is only a convenient phrase of the man of science, and is generally used without a thought of what it signifies. The truth is that this is only a name for something else. There can be no such thing as force independent of personality, either finite or infinite, and the final fact of all science and philosophy and theology and revelation is that, instead of there being many forces which we are wont to call natural and impersonal, there is but one force, and that is spiritual and personal. The forces of nature are nothing else than the immanent God. The force that drives the planets in their course, the force that holds us to the earth and holds the earth together, the force that keeps the minutest particle of matter intact and gives it identity, the force that drives the locomotive and propels the wheels of factories and commerce, the force that carries the message so mysteriously along the wire and across the sea, the force that flashes so instantaneously from other planets to our own across multiplied millions of miles, the force that bears up the clouds and sends down the shower, the force that bursts the shell and sprouts the seed, that develops the plant and the tree and paints the beauties of the flower and the fruit, every force of the world and the universe, except that of man and whatever other finite beings there may be, is the activity of the infinite God; and the law of the force's activity is nothing else than the immutable course of divine wisdom in giving to the world order and system.

It is God then who reigns, instead of laws and forces. He is so intimately identified with the world, and the world is so dependent upon him, that should he for one moment cease to act, all things but himself would cease to be. His continual activity in the material world is so essential to its existence, that his active presence amounts to a continuous creation. But whether finite personalities are by nature so persistent as to continue to exist eternally, without moral and vital union with the infinite Source of life, is a question of philosophic speculation and Biblical interpretation on which the greatest minds and best hearts of the world differ. For the final answer to this solemn question we shall have to wait. We are at present concerned with the mysteries of this world under the reign of infinite Beneficence.

If, then, we are to think of the infinitely

wise and good God, instead of natural
forces working in the world, do we not indict him for all the death and devastation
that follow in the path of these forces when
they are awake and mad with fury? Tor-
nadoes and earthquakes and floods and con-
flagrations and wrecks and thunderbolts
are instances of the violence of these natural forces, which also play havoc in ten
thousand other ways all over the world.
Are we to think, then, that instead of natural forces, it is God who is doing all this?
The question is reasonable and to the point.
We answer in the affirmative, but ask the
patience and careful consideration of the
reader before he allows his nature to revolt
at the thought.

The fact is, this world is composed of
two hemispheres, the bright and the dark.
We like to think of and live in the bright
side of life, but we are all forced to feel
and see the dark side also, and it is this
that gives us trouble and despair. We can

not get rid of the darkness, nor can we get rid of the thought that some one is responsible for it. But when we say that God reigns in this world, we do not indict him for any of its evils. He reigns, but his throne is white. His government is beneficent.

Much of the horror which we feel on account of accidents and catastrophies is due to circumstances. The farther they are removed from us in time and place and personal significance, the less distressing are they to us. The burning and burying of Pompeii by the eruption of Mt. Vesuvius in the year 79 shocks us less than the ruin of the city of St. Pierre by the eruption of Mt. Pelee nineteen centuries later. The drowning of thousands in China by the overflow of a river impresses us less deeply than the Johnstown or Galveston horror in our own land. The death of multitudes in a single disaster is more horrifying than the death of many times that number, if

4

they take place by individuals in as many different places and from different causes. Death from accident seems worse than death from a lingering disease. And when our loved ones are taken from us our hearts are broken, though the death of a stranger is little more than a passing event.

But aside from the extreme horror that we feel on account of circumstances attending the calamities of the world, the fact still remains that all men are sufferers in some way or another, and none are exempt from that final separation that breaks all the ties that bind us to this world and to those we so much love. The whole problem then reduced to its simplest form is this: Why should God so govern the world and so deal with men as to cause any one ever to suffer or die? The question is a reasonable one, but it can not be answered in a few words.

Only two kinds of worlds are conceivable. One is the world that we have—a

world of order and system, created and
governed by a presiding Mind. The other
is an impossible world that is created in
the human imagination, a world all topsy-
turvy, harum-scarum. But if this were a
topsy-turvy world: if to-day a given body
weighed three or four times as much as it
did yesterday, if we never could tell
whether an unsupported body would fall
to the ground or ascend into the air, if to-
day the temperature should be one hundred
degrees and to-morrow forty degrees below
zero, if at one time a certain vegetable were
food and at another time poison, if the normal temperature of the human body varied
with the changes in atmospheric temperature, if one day were ten hours long and
another fifteen and another twenty-five, if
seasons did not come and go in any fixed
routine, if, in short, we could never be sure
of anything, our lives and even our mental
and moral powers would be overthrown.
We therefore need and must have a world

in which there is a fixed order and one upon which we can with confidence depend. Hence God acts uniformly in the world for our highest good. His ways of working are laws of life for us, though they may and often do occasion suffering and death. But if we stand across the path which his wisdom and goodness take in working out for us our highest good, the consequence should not be charged to the sovereign severity of God.

It seems then both reasonable and right that a fixed and reliable order should be maintained in this world, and that immunity from suffering and death should not be expected either as a reward for great piety and devotion, or because of God's compassion toward human ignorance and weakness or childish innocence and mistakes.

If we are to pass judgment on what God does with us and for us, we must keep in mind his evident purpose in all that he does. And if we should think there is a better way than his, we must test it also by the effect it would have upon us.

If in our judgment only the wicked and vicious should suffer and the devout and virtuous be exempt, we should not forget that there are numberless degrees of character in the descending scale from the best to the worst, and that each of us is judged in a different light by every other man. The same is true of the degree of strength and of knowledge that one may have. If, then, God should grant immunity from suffering according to the degree of merit that each man possesses, it is easy to see that the effect upon all would be confusing and demoralizing. There would be no established order in the course of nature, and nothing could be depended upon with the assurance of safety. Such would be the effect upon us of any way than that which is. God's way is the best and only possible way. Any other would end in confusion and disaster to mental and moral life.

God reigns. It is not impersonal, powerless natural laws, or blind, irresponsible natural forces that reign. Neither is it a demon or any number of demons who reign either absolutely or as God's rivals. God alone reigns. The evils for which we hold some superior evil power responsible are not all such. The amount of evil that actually exists in the world varies with the larger or the more limited views that men take of the world and life and duty and God and destiny. The small soul who thinks and lives for himself alone, deals with the devil continually, and sees his mischief in everything and everybody. He thinks of the devil more than he does of God, and sees God's hand less in the affairs of men than he does the strong arm of a rival power. It is quite different with the man who is godlike, unselfish, and devout. The devil is of little importance to him personally; he holds no important place in his creed, and in no sense does he reign as God's rival in the world. But he thinks of God, holds fellowship with him, and rejoices to recognize his reign over the whole earth, through his entire universe and from age to age, eternally. The man who has the larger vision sees things more in God's light and recognizes the beneficence of his government more fully. He does not make the common mistake of limiting God's government to the physical world, and his purpose to the progress of the order of nature. He sees that the supreme purpose of God and the end toward which he is working in all things is a moral one. Viewing the world as moral, even in the physical realm, most of its mysteries that are of a moral nature are dissolved, and beneficence completely floods the mind's horizon with its consolation and holy light.

God reigns, and his throne is white. It is never, never usurped by an evil power or abdicated for his misuse. Upon it there

is no stain of cruelty or injustice or un-
kindness. No weakness or indifference or
partiality is conceivable in his sovereignty.
His scepter never trembles. In wisdom
and righteousness and strength, boundless
and everlasting, he reigns King of kings
and Lord of lords.

CHAPTER IV.

DIVINE PURPOSE.

It is not unreasonable to think that God governs this world chiefly in the interest of the moral or spiritual, rather than the physical or natural order. It is reasonable to believe that he prizes virtue, holiness, love, intelligence, courage, freedom, and the like more highly than he does the characteristics of natural objects; that men who can think his thoughts after him, respond to the heart-throbs of eternal love and pity, and follow the devious path that leads through darkness upward to the light are by him esteemed more highly than mountains, though they be filled with treasures of gold; that nations are worth more to him than continents; and the moral universe than suns and systems without number.

57

Even in the realm of physical facts this
is more a moral than it is a material world.
Creation was a moral act of God bringing
into existence an arena for the activities
of moral beings, to whom life would be
sweet and achievement a delight.   The
maintenance of the world is likewise a
moral process with a moral end in view.
In the realization of this end the one
changeless fact is the moral purpose of
God.   This is as certainly unalterable as
his moral nature.   In the realization of his
purpose he makes the natural order a
means; and, while his purpose never varies,
his method of working it out may and does
change.   As nature is only a method, so
far as we can see, and not an end, there
have been variations from a fixed order
for the purpose of realizing higher ends
than can be realized in a material system.

Variations in the natural order are necessary for the accomplishment of God's
purpose, which is the perfection of moral

beings and ultimately a moral world. But these variations are only exceptions in a fixed natural order, and not the order itself. Both the variations and the established order are necessary for the development of a moral world and the fulfillment of God's righteous will.

The security of life, as well as the balance of our reason and our moral nature, require stability in the order of the world. We are so closely bound to nature and so dependent upon it, that its course must be sufficiently regular and wholly reliable. Its laws must be, as they are, laws of life to us. But should there never be any variation from a fixed, inflexible order in nature, the purpose of God in perfecting in us our higher, moral nature would be defeated. The requirements of our bodies are so immediate, so imperative, and so numerous, that it is necessary for our good that there should be windows through the hard, dark wall of inexorable law and unsympathizing nature to let in light from the spiritual world. For were it not for such light from above we would think that nature is all, that we are of the earth ourselves, that our duty is to nature alone, and that when it affords no light we must walk in darkness, and when it gives no consolation we must in sorrow bow to our fate.

It is therefore for our highest good that God does at times do things in a way different from the ordinary course which we see in nature. These variations in his method of working are what we call miracles. As an illustration, if we saw all the water in one of the great lakes suddenly rise from its basin in one vast volume and thus be lifted to the clouds, we should call it the most impressive miracle the world has ever known. But the miraculousness of it would be in its variation from the ordinary; for, in fact, that much water is raised to the clouds every day by the natural method of evaporation. Were one way as common as the other, we should probably think the latter method of evaporation the most remarkable and mysterious, as it would be. The method which was the greatest break in the course of natural law, we should call the miraculous.

But with God there is no such thing as a miracle. That which is changeless is his moral purpose, and both the ordinary, which we call natural, and the extraordinary, which we call supernatural, are methods by which he works his beneficent will, and only methods. All the time he is acting on the high moral plane of directing the thoughts of men to himself, whom they should adoringly fear and lovingly obey for the good it will be to them. When he wishes to declare the authority of a prophet or an apostle as a messenger of truth to the world and to all ages, he does through him, or, in the presence of witnesses, does something himself, which shall stand out as a great historic fact. But should these wonders become common daily happenings, the purpose of God to awaken and perfect the moral natures of men would be defeated as certainly as it would be if they never occurred at all.

This truth sheds light on the dark problems of the world and life. We wonder why God does not more frequently interpose and avert disaster, dispel darkness, and relieve suffering. But, if any, why not all? And if all, would his moral purpose be realized in us and in the world? If when the seas are swept by storms that imperil the lives of voyagers, every captain of an ocean liner were given power to stand on deck, and, stretching forth his hand, speak to the tempest, "Peace, be still," and it should obey him as the storm on Galilee obeyed the Master; if God should feed the famine-stricken districts of Asia with manna as he did the Israelites in the wilderness; if in answer to prayer an approaching cyclone should be turned back

or be lifted to spare a city, and then sweep
on in its destructive course; if the pious
and the innocent alone were made invulner-
able to the thunderbolt; if at will any one,
following his heart of sympathy, might
open the eyes of the blind, cause the lame
to walk, or raise sufferers from their sick-
beds to comfort and health; if when our
loved ones die we could take some sympa-
thizing friend with us to where they lay
who should be able with a word to call them
forth and restore them to us alive, loving,
and true; if by a word, a stroke of the
hand, a prayer, or by gifts or sacrifices
however costly we could realize all our
fond desires for ourselves or for others,
would the world be better off than it is?
Surely not. Instead of order we should
have confusion. Instead of a God whom
we could trust, we should have one whom
we could not regard. Instead of being impressed by the divine interposition, we
should be as insensible and irreverent as

rocks. Instead of God's purpose being realized in us, it would end in failure. What
we need is sufficient light shining into
our dark abode to inspire us all with the
sweeter, purer light of heaven, and that
much is given. If we had more it would be
no better to us than the shining of the sun
or the pale, still light of the moon.

Again, since the happiness and hope of
the world depend so much upon our having
a full knowledge of great, fundamental
truths, children that we are, we do not see
why God does not use his authority in giving to all the world a full-orbed knowledge
of all that we need to know. If wisdom
and goodness were not his attributes also,
it would not be hard to see that by his almightiness he could give to all nations just
such a revelation. He could make every
cloud his Shekinah by day and by night.
He could write his law in letters of fire
upon the curtain of the sky. He could
cause every thunderbolt to articulate his

righteous wrath against all iniquity. He could inscribe upon every leaf of forest and field his message of mercy to the meek and lowly of heart. He could make every gentle breeze whisper in our ears his fatherly love for all his children. He could startle every sinner from his lethargy and stop him in his course of self-destruction by writing upon the wall of his house of feasting and debauchery and shame, "Thou art weighed in the balance and found wanting." He could give to the waves that ever beat upon the sands and rocks of an endless shore the voice that tells of immortality, and cause the rolling ocean to respond with the solemn significance of eternity. He could raise up prophets and send them to all people and tongues, giving them as their divine credentials the power to do miracles and mighty works. The possibilities of God's almightiness to give to the whole world a perfect revelation certainly are without limit.

5

But with such a revelation, full and universal, would the world be any better off than it is? So it may seem to some. Instead of having the many existing forms of false and conflicting religions, we should have had from the first the one true religion, and the worship of the one and only true God. We never should have had the true religion rent by doctrinal controversies, as it has been. Holy wars, persecutions, inquisitorial tribunals, intolerance, strife, and enmity would have been unknown in history, because the light of divine truth had shone always everywhere. We should have been free from all modern religious fads and heresies. The age-long conflicts of science and religion, and of Christianity and free thought would have been impossible, because nature and revelation would have been manifestly harmonious and evidently of one origin, and that divine. Atheism would have been a thing unknown, for God's existence would

have been a self-evident fact to every mind
and clear as a sunbeam. Agnosticism
would have been equally impossible, for the
knowledge of him and all fundamental
truth would have been as certain as the
consciousness of one's own existence.
There would have been no place for natu-
ralism, because all effects in nature would
have been directly traceable to the one
great Cause of all things. Positivism
never would have had a name, for knowledge would have been so direct that the
truth would not have been a tax either on
one's logic in proving it, or on one's faith
in believing it. Our origin, duty, and destiny would have been so revealed that there
could have remained no room for doubt or
misgiving or fear or despair. But such a
revelation as this God has not given. And
yet the wish that it had been made is im-
plied in all our childish impatience with
Providence.

The desire that we have to know the mysteries of the world and to have the highest good realized in all men is a divine trait in us, instead of a reflection upon our great heartedness and love of humanity. But how utterly fatal to the divine purpose for the world would our wishes be, were they substituted for the method which God pursues in the world!

Should the extraordinary become continuous, should the supernatural become common, it would be no more impressive than nature alone would be. In fact, the natural and the supernatural would be to us identical. If the revelation were made as universal and inflexible as nature, the world would be reduced to an order in which there would, after all, be no supernatural element. And if, on the other hand, the revelation were universal, but subject to no order or system, we should have a world of disorder which would wreck all reason as well as faith. In either case the divine purpose to awaken and develop the moral life of the world by impressions from the spiritual world would fail.

Another fact must not be overlooked. Man is not a mechanism. He does not receive truth passively, then give it forth in the form of character and influence, as the water receives the sunlight, then reflects it back toward its source. However, there is something more the matter with the world than the need of greater knowledge, unless it be that knowledge which is equivalent to wisdom, in which there is a due regard for moral excellence. Hence, were it morally possible for God to give to all mankind a clear revelation of himself, a full knowledge of their divine obligations, a definite code of social ethics and standards of national and world righteousness, there would still be lacking the necessary moral impulse and love of true godliness to raise the truth thus revealed into the living form of personal excellence. Infinite wisdom has given tc the world all the light it has needed. Not all the light that perfect knowledge calls for, but all that perfect moral development requires, and this is God's purpose concerning us, and our supreme need.

A revelation, even though it were as universal as nature itself, would therefore not take out of the world its cruelty and crime, its intolerance and ignorance, its doubt and despair. The spread of Gospel light in the Christian nations did not put an end to wars and persecutions and intolerance. It did not settle the controversies of creeds and put an end to all heresy. The world was morally wrong, and when the right goes forth in a world of wrong there will be war and suffering until righteousness, which has the right of way, is triumphant everywhere. Contradictory as it may seem, the Prince of Peace came not to bring peace on earth, but a sword. But peace will come to earth when good-will to men becomes a universal practice in the world. That is, when the moral purpose of God is realized.

Disbelief has ever been due to disposition, far more than to the need of greater light. Men are atheists, agnostics, materialists, anything and everything in Christian lands, with open Bible in hand and with evidences on every side of God's presence and power in the world.

The cure of disbelief and doubt, and their consequent suffering and despair, is an honest attitude of will and affection toward the truth that God has given, and toward himself as the infinite power in the world who works for righteousness.

Nor has God shown favoritism, in that he has withheld the higher forms of revelation from some nations and given it to others, and in making it more clear in these Christian centuries than he did in the morning centuries of history. Excessive light

would have been blinding rather than il-
luminating to ages and nations in great
darkness. The moral life of the world, the
same as of the individual, is a development.
As the moral life unfolds, the apprehension
of the truth revealed becomes more clear.
Then the higher and more spiritual forms
of revelation are imparted. The form and
the degree that the revelation takes are always justified by the end that God has in
view for the world and the capacity of the
world at any given time to understand
what he would make known to it. But if
all the world has not and never did have
the sacred Scriptures, this does not mean
that any part of the world has ever been
abandoned by God to utter darkness and
hopelessness. The fact that in every age
all nations have had some form of religious
worship, though it may be most degrading
homage paid to incarnations of passion
and vice, and the fact also that these nations have ever felt after God, if happily

sympathy and works of mercy embrace all men the world over.

These facts of miracle and prophecy as methods of God in working out his holy will in the world point to another fact which is infinitely more significant than any other for the world's hope and happiness; namely, the incarnation of the Son of God. Here is the miracle that is greater than all other miracles, for he is the most unaccountable fact in all history from the standpoint of one who would account for him as he may account for other men. For other men, no matter how high they may rise above their age, can be accounted for by antecedent forces and surrounding influences. They may be great enough to be called remarkable men, and go down as historic characters. But Christ can not be accounted for as other men are. For, while he rose infinitely above his own age and could not have been the product of a race of antecedents, he is so superior to other men that he rises far above any who have appeared in the world since his time. So pure, so universal, so great is he, that he is the human type for all ages and nations, and the prophecy in person of the perfected purpose of God for humanity. He is a complete break in the series of natural causes. He appears in the world through the veil of nature; still he is not of natural origin. So far superior is he to nature, that it yields to his word and touch as though it recognized in him its rightful Lord.

Christ is the most unaccountable historic fact known to men. He has arrested the thought of the world and captivated its heart more effectually than all other facts. He is a miracle even in the sphere of the miraculous, a supernatural fact in the course of supernatural events. His mission to the world was to reveal not only God to men, but to reveal men to themselves, and to point all men to what they are capable of being by God's purpose concerning them becoming realized.

The Incarnation is therefore not an end in itself, but is the supreme act of God in his method of working out his will in men and the world. Of all facts that rise above nature into the class of the supernatural, the most impressive is the presence of the Son of God in the world, partaking of human flesh and blood, but living a life, revealing a character, setting in motion moral forces, and teaching truths fundamental for all ages and nations. He came into the world in the fullness of time, when the world was ready for him, and he went out of the world when he did, because he knew it was expedient for him to go. One Christ is all that the world has had, and all that it ever shall need. Upon him, through the Spirit's universal influence, the minds of men will ever be fixed, and the better he is known and trusted, the more will the wrongs of the world be righted, the hearts of men be purified, and their lives glorified. Never will his moral magnetism diminish or his light grow dim.

Christ came into the world to do the will of his Father who sent him, and, having finished the work that he gave him to do, he disappeared from the sight of men, that through the Spirit he might become a universal Christ and remain with us always, even unto the end of the world.

What shall we say then? Are not God's thoughts and ways as high as the heavens above our thoughts and our ways? His purpose is infinitely wise and good, and his method of working it out through miracle, prophecy, the Incarnation, the Spirit's inspiration, and providence is likewise divinely beneficent.

Darkness is not all dissolved, suffering is not all alleviated, tears are not all wiped away, wrong is not all righted, his ways are not all known; but the moral world is only in the formative period yet. The perfect has not yet been realized. But it is God's plan that it shall be. Through all the variations that come in the course of

history and the process of nature, as well
as in the more permanent order, where,
as a rule, events come to pass according to
fixed law, the one factor universal and eternal is God's moral law. From it there is
never a shadow of turning. It is his unalterable method of achieving his final purpose in the world.

There is divine moral purpose in every
event, every fact, every experience, everything. The patient, truth-seeking soul will
try to trace this purpose in all the onward
movements of the world. He will not
hastily conclude from this or that fact what
that purpose is, much less will he doubt
such a purpose because of mystery or calamity or suffering. If he can not understand, he nevertheless will believe that God
is good and wise, and to him this is better
than sight; it is the substance of the things
for which he hopes, the evidence of things
which otherwise can not be known.

6

CHAPTER V.

The Race Under Discipline.

The wretchedness of the race through all the centuries of its slow progress to its present state of peace, enlightenment, and righteousness has caused many to doubt even a race providence, not to mention a divine care for the individual.

It must be confessed that the history of the world is a sad, dark story viewed in the light of the physical and moral misery which the race has borne in its desperate, blind struggle toward civilization. But there is no ground for indicting God as the cause of it. His reign over the earth and in all human affairs has ever been beneficent, wise, and just. His throne has been stainless and white. If the race, like a current of water, flowed on in a prescribed course guided by external forces which were sufficient to explain all its movements and varied conditions, then there might be some possible ground for charging the world's woes to faults and failures in God's government; he could have made human existence brighter and better, but did not. But if man was to be what he is, and not something so passive, impressionless, and irresponsible as to be a different order of being altogether, then no course of providence is conceivable which would have hastened the race with greater speed and certainty toward its appointed goal.

Man was made for action and achievement, and the earth an arena for his valor. If, then, the race has found the world to contain more mystery than plain truth, it does not follow that God is jealous of knowledge in his creatures. If there were given to man heavy burdens to bear, and a long, hard journey to travel over an unknown and devious path, this does not mean

that existence begins and ends with toil,
or that there is no compensation at last for
his weariness and burden-bearing. And if
there has been bleeding and suffering in all
ages, the conclusion is not that the God
who is over all and blessed forever is a dis-
interested observer of all this terrible
strife, or that he looks upon the agony of
the world with no heart of pity and no
hand of help.

We are to think of the race which is,
and not an imaginary one; a race which,
though very imperfect, is capable, through
discipline, of development to a state of perfection which far transcends our utmost
present conception; and for such a purpose
this is the best possible world, and God's
method of instruction and discipline is the
best, no doubt, that infinite wisdom and
goodness could devise; certainly better
than human ingenuity could plan.

It is quite true that for aught we know
the material world and the course of nature

may serve even a higher purpose than being a field for human valor and achievement. We do not know what significance it may have for the Creator himself, beyond the purpose it may serve the human race. It may possibly be of more service to man after he has passed beyond the shadows of earth and time and joined the innumerable company of immortals, than it was while he made it his home and school for mental and moral discipline. For the material universe certainly contains mysteries deep enough and numerous to tax the minds of loftier spirits and more divine than can be attributed to human souls in this world, however perfect they may be in mental grasp and spiritual insight, and it may serve such beings as its chief end. But such ideas can be only conjectural. We are not in a position to see that nature serves any purpose higher than being an arena for man's discipline and development while he is living in this world.

And it certainly has served this purpose well. For, whichever view one may hold as to man's primitive state, whether that of a high degree of intelligence, clear understanding of social rights and duties, lofty ideals, pure morals, spiritual perception, or that of an undeveloped savage; whether he be regarded as allied to his Creator or to the beast of the field, we certainly find that, from the beginning of reliable history to the present, there has been a race progress upward and away from the selfish and the animal toward the social and the moral life. The world was new and the race was young, just the kind of a world that the young race needed. There were unsailed seas, unexplored continents, undiscovered resources, unknown laws, unseen forces, undeveloped principles, and unclassified facts. The task of turning the desert world into a thing of service and beauty was given to man. But had his wants all been so well supplied as to re-

quire no effort upon his part to obtain
them; had he from the beginning been
made free from drudgery and disease and
suffering and death; had the world been a
thing so small and so simple as to call
forth no activity and require no courage;
had he been made so perfect in his mental
and moral nature as to find no mysteries
in the world to master, no secrets to solve,
and no trials to test him; had his social
nature been fully developed so that each
man knew and owned every other man as
his brother and felt himself to be his
keeper; had he freely acquiesced in governments and laws and language and science and philosophy and religion and all
forms of truth given to him perfected by
God at the beginning; had his own nature
been fully developed and he able fully to
understand the world of mystery that is in
his own soul, what would have been the
result? Evidently this: The race would

have died in infancy, and the earth would have remained a waste place unto this day.

It is not hard to recognize a race providence, while we think only of the agreeable things and the visible hand of God in the world. We can all easily believe and be optimistic in our faith while we look only on the bright side of the world's life. It is when the darkness overtakes us that we are seized with despair and doubt. It is when we reflect upon the groveling, groping, wretchedness, and helplessness of the race and of "man's inhumanity to man" that we wonder where God is and what interest he has in the world's happiness and progress. There is a "soul of goodness in things evil," but it is not always manifest, and when for the want of a true faith and a clear spiritual insight we are unable to see it, we seize upon the "things evil," and then our sense of what is right and just leads us to question a beneficence in the world-order. Nevertheless there is a world-providence even in the things which seem to be incompatible with a beneficent and faultless moral government among men.

The physical features of the earth show plainly that God intended it, not as a pleasure ground for men, but as a place of discipline. Some men are so extremely utilitarian that they can see no good reason why such a large part of the earth's surface should be composed of vast regions of snow and ice, broad ocean wastes, storm-swept, dreary deserts, and rock-ribbed mountains. But these have been the natural boundaries and bulwarks for the nations through all the centuries. For this reason they have served a beneficent purpose in protecting the race from its own suicidal hand. For, had it not been for these natural barriers which made the transportation or march of armies from one country to another difficult, if not in many instances impossible, those nations

which have given to the world the richest
treasures of art, language, culture, and
religion, and some of the highest ideals of
national and domestic life, would have been
exterminated in their infancy. Moreover,
it seems that God kept the richest continents a secret from the race by these vast
wastes of water and sand and ice, and re-
served them until he had trained peoples
who were courageous and worthy enough
to go over and possess them, and there
raise the ensign of freedom and protection
for the downtrodden multitudes of earth.
To some it may seem that fertile plains,
stately forests, rivers of oil, mountains of
minerals, and hills of granite and marble
would have served the world far better
than these vast uninhabitable and unpro-
ductive areas. But such a view is too nar-
row to commend itself to the thoughtful.
God has abundantly provided the race with
all these things, and they serve, as far as
they are capable of serving, the purpose of

God in training the race in righteousness and helping it to a happy existence.

But it is not in great riches and resources that any age or people is strong and great. The world's richest treasures are its moral and intellectual fiber and productiveness. If then these vast wastes have served the purpose of protecting the race from self-destruction; if in surmounting them it has been trained in character and courage; if they have created brain and brawn; if they have fostered freedom and faith; if the cities built by the seas have been beautified with the highest arts and the noblest architecture; if in these cities have been founded the schools in which the world's masters have developed and taught the systems of truth which have been the inspiration and the light of the ages; if conquering commerce and political greatness have followed the circle of the seas; if the greatest achievements in structural engineering have been the products of nations hemmed in by natural barriers; if all this wealth has become the world's possession on account of the inspiration, protection, influence, and discipline of des- erts and mountains and seas and zones of snow and ice, then who can say that the race has not been better cared for than it would have been with infinite resources of material wealth and physical comfort?

Those who are unable to see that the barrenness of so large a part of the earth's surface can serve any good end for the race, should remember that all those little imperial powers of thought and energy and faith, such as Palestine, Greece, Italy, Hol- land, Great Britain, and New England, where the world's heart has throbbed deep- est, and the stream of divine life has flowed fastest and fullest, have been situated where lofty mountains, broad deserts, or rolling, restless seas have awakened thoughts of the infinite and have created courage in the race's struggle for existence. From this point of view they will see less occasion of finding fault with God's government and more clearly recognize his moral purpose in the training of the race.

Again, we are just beginning to see how exhaustless are the physical forces and material resources of the world, and the uses which they serve in uniting all people in ties of intelligence and fraternity, in lifting burdens from the backs of men and beasts, and in multiplying the comforts and unfolding the moral life of mankind. We are just in the early dawn of the last day of creation, the Sabbath of the world's rest. The forces and the resources of nature, which God garnered up ages upon ages ago for the future service and comfort of the race, are just beginning to relieve the weariness of toiling hands and tired feet. Relieved of many of their heavy physical burdens, men are beginning to have strength and time for other and higher tasks. They may now give attention to the culture of mind and heart. They may develop their ethical and social lives and add to their domestic and religious joys.

Nature is certainly a rich storehouse of treasures and forces and laws for the benefit of the race, but why were its doors for so many ages shut and its contents kept a profound secret? Why should man have to till the soil with a stick or stone until a few generations ago, while the very dirt in which he dug contained iron for implements that would have made his toil lighter and his harvest more abundant? Why was he so long ignorant of the use of coal to drive the wheels of commerce and manufacturing, and these great world industries be so long retarded on account of it? Why was the use of steam, one of the mightiest forces in nature, a thing unknown to the race until recently, though its presence in the world has for ages been a matter of common knowledge? Electricity has ever offered its services to lift the burdens from

man and beast and bless the world with its
language and light, but strangely enough
the ages have stupidly feared its voice and
known not its good-will. And why should
disease and suffering ravage the race so
long, while remedies for the relief of so
many human ills abounded everywhere?

The blessings of providence that have
been stored up in this old time-worn earth
and have long waited and still wait the
world's service are numberless. But why
was not the race made aware of the use of
all these elements and powers that enter
into the arts and sciences of civilized life
long ages ago? Why did not the Hand that
placed them here disclose their secret and
put them to the service of a suffering, helpless world in its childhood? And if a better day is coming on, a day of universal
sympathy and comfort and peace and
brotherhood, because of a better knowledge
of what God has done to bless mankind,
why must millions still suffer and toil on

and die while the world continues to grope for greater light?

Such questions can reasonably be raised only as we imagine the earth to be filled with a race of beings other than men, or think of God as dealing so arbitrarily with men as utterly to ignore what they really are and treating them as though they were things instead. If the race were composed of beings who could have no appreciation of providence, no sense of duty, no choice of right, no fear of penalty, no sense of responsibility, no aspiration for goodness, no power of reason, who, in short, are wholly incapable of development, then there would be some justification for finding fault with God's way of dealing with them. But such creatures would not be men.

Upon the other hand, if God could take men as they are and exalt them by his almighty power to such a state of perfection as would make them insensible to suffering,

and give them a clear knowledge of all
facts and laws and duties and perfect their
moral and social natures and give them
composure of heart and rest of faith in his
good providence and submission to his
wholesome discipline, but did not do so,
then we might again complain justly that
he was not doing his best to improve the
condition of his dependent children. But
such a thing would be an impossibility even
with almighty God. For, should he thus
raise man arbitrarily to such a state of ex-
altation he would be destroying man and
making a being of another order.

It is the race of beings which we call
men that God is dealing with and disciplining, and for it he is working wisely,
as best he can, to bring it to its appointed
beneficent goal. The Spirit of God has
ever brooded over the chaos of humanity,
bringing light out of darkness, order out
of confusion, good out of evil, and happiness out of sorrow and suffering; and he

7

will continue to co-operate with the struggling race as it strives to rise until his moral purpose for the world is fully realized. But in his guardianship over the world God has followed the course of discipline that has developed the race symmetrically. For it is with the race as it is with the individual; the method of instruction followed must recognize the capacity to receive and use the gifts of God, and the stages of instruction must progress from the lower to the higher.

Now, the goal of the world is a moral one, and the movement of the race as a whole has ever been toward that end. But such is the character of undeveloped humanity that it would have been fatal to have put it in possession of the wealth and forces and privileges of modern civilization before men and nations became sufficiently rational and moral to use them judiciously. Had barbarous ages been put in possession of modern means of transportation and modern instruments of warfare, had they known the chemistry of explosives and the varied uses of electricity, had they been familiar with the geography of the earth and the languages of hostile tribes, the slaughter of savage and semi-civilized nations would have been well-nigh complete, and the world's progress would have been retarded. There would have been vastly more suffering than there has been from the plan and the program of providence for the world.

No good has God ever denied the world when the fullness of time had come for the world to receive and enjoy it; for no blessing, however great, is ever fit for man's use until man is fit to use it. The knowledge of great truths, the use of great forces, the service of great riches, all come in the course of human progress and constitute progress, though strangely enough about every great discovery or idea or reform has had its crucified lord. Who then can justify any objection to the way God has withheld from former ages any of the blessings which this age of civilization enjoys?

Another thing which looks like divine indifference concerning the good of the race, is the small degree of knowledge which the present age possesses of the people and civilization of the early centuries of the world's history. If each age is rightful heir to all the good of the ages that went before it, why did not the great Teacher and Benefactor of the world preserve for coming generations all the arts and literature and laws and customs and religious light of the pioneer peoples of the world that are now dead and forgotten? Why have they not signified more for the world of to-day? Did God care so little for the latter ages as not to preserve for them the early records of the race, or did he consider the achievements of the ages of oblivion to be of so little consequence for the future? By excavating the buried ruins of ancient cities, desecrating the tombs of dead nations, deciphering hieroglyphics, translating scraps of time-worn parchment, crediting truth to the traditions and legends and myths that have been handed down from generation to generation, digging up old coins and broken columns, and making all that we can of every chance discovery that bears the marks of antiquity, we have found that the nations now lost to reliable history are by no means to be despised for what they achieved.

But even if what they did achieve signified but little in comparison with the marvels of the present century, it is of interest to us that we know something more definite than we do of the first scenes and actors of the age-long drama of man. It seems right, too, that we should know who our early benefactors were, that we may better revere their memory. But they are dead, and what they did is buried with

them. Why has God so dealt with the
race? The only true answer is that he has
done so for the training and perfecting of
a race of intelligent moral beings.

In the first place, truth is not of human
origin. All truth is eternal, and when it
becomes a matter of human knowledge it
is either from discovery or revelation, or
both; and when it becomes known, it remains forever the world's possession. It
may be handed down from age to age and
pass from nation to nation, and in its
course take on new forms, but the substance of it never dies or disappears from
the world. It is ever appearing and reap-
pearing in a new light, and often in such
a changed appearance as to be identified
with difficulty. And yet it is the same time-
honored truth. In his education of the
race God does not burden men with non-
essentials, the minor details and forms of
truth, but inspires them with the essentials,
the fundamentals, the living realities.

Truth has life, and whatever the ancient world may have known of it still lives. It survives customs, language, literature, religion, caste, tribal characteristics, storms of revolution, and the death of nations. It is heaven-born, and in an upper current passes along from age to age.

It is not possible for us to analyze the infinitely complex stream of truth that courses through and constitutes our present civilization. No man is able to tell when and by whom one-thousandth part of the truth which he may know came to be the world's possession. That is a matter of little consequence to him. To know that he knows it, without knowing its history, is enough. Much less is it possible to trace all the world's truth back to where it was born from above. This is not necessary for our happiness and progress. For this reason God has buried the dead past, but given a resurrection unto life of the soul of ancient civilization and culture, and the soul of it is our heritage to-day.

Comparatively little has God given to man ready for his use and easy of access, but he has done for him what is infinitely more for his good. He has placed him in a world where facts are sown broadcast, where forces clash, where struggle for existence is the law of life, where truth is but partly revealed, where only the still small voice of the Creator is heard, where all conceivable mysteries about the past and all degrees of uncertainty about the future exist, where want and grief and suffering and death abound, where everything is changing and transitory, where all conceivable forms of religion and caste and superstition abound along with race prejudice and varied degrees of national morality and enlightenment. He has placed him in this kind of a world for a good and wise purpose, and that purpose has been in process of realization through all the ages.

These are the things that have awakened
the curiosity of mankind, invited investi-
gation, challenged endeavor, tested endur-
ance, developed brawn and brain, humbled
pride, purified life, established faith, culti-
vated philanthropy, and united the race
ever more in the firmer bonds of peace and
good-will.

It is not luxury and laxity of discipline
that have advanced the race. It is the ob-
stacles in the way of progress and life and
happiness that defy, and for the most part
defeat, that have disciplined the race and
have made man the master that he is.

Governments, laws, industrial society,
social life, international comity, the home,
the family, the school, the Church, and all
the institutions of Christian civilization exist to bless mankind, because both the ne-
cessity of them and the desire for them
were implanted in human nature, and because God has ever worked in the race,
both to will and to do of his good pleasure.

and religion, united with morality, is reign-
ing more and more in the consciences of
the nations. The laws of God are becoming the laws of the people. Brotherhood is
binding together the ends of the earth.
Philosophy and science and industry and
literature and laws and civil government
and social, state, and Church institutions
are becoming allied with the truth of revelation, and the giant men of the great nations of earth are owning the Christ as
Master and Lord.

But the will of God is not yet done
in earth as it is done in heaven. There
have been wars, revolutions, persecutions,
black atrocities, foul injustice, enervat-
ing wealth, luxury, and laxity in morals,
and history is likely to repeat itself.
The world is entering upon an age of
Christian enlightenment. The righteousness of almighty God has the right of
way in the earth, but as it goes forth in a
world of wrong its rights are sure to be

face from the ends of the earth, and the epoch be one manifesting the might and the wisdom and the goodness of the Judge of all the earth. The nations shall see God and adore.

The human race believes both in God and in its high calling. This is the phillosophy of its history and progress. The first article of the universal creed is the idea of God. It is universal because it belongs in human nature. It is not born of fear or dreams. Animals fear and evidently dream, but they know and feel and believe nothing of God, because there is not that within them that answers to the infinite Being who created them. But God has made man to know him and feel his presence in the world. The fact of God without and the idea of God within answer to each other. This realized relationship is the inspiration of the race and the spring of its progress. Where the conception of God has been the highest, the inspiration opening for recognition. It forces nations to face each other with the best that they have of everything, moral, social, industrial, civil, and religious, and the Lord God of Hosts, who is over every battlefield, above each monarch's throne, in every council of peace, causes his truth to triumph, his name to be known.

Day is just dawning on the Dark Continent. A rim of light circles its horizon with a promise of the morning. Heralds of the Cross have brought the light that shall brighten ever until its age-long night is turned to eternal day. But what shall be the history of its civilization? So situated geographically as to be equally accessible to the nations of America, Europe, and Asia, Africa is destined to be the field of conflict for the great powers of three continents. Here again faith and superstition, justice and greed, truth and error, humanity and barbarism, the Author of life and the idols of death shall again come face to

East. The Eastern Question, in which the interests of the nations of the earth, as well as the religions of all mankind, are involved, is the greatest that has ever come to the race as a whole for solution. It is to be hoped that it will be settled peaceably and justly, but that is too much to expect. It is more probable that its history when written will be one of the most terrible chapters in the annals of the world. Nations in which Christianity has given tone to diplomacy and temper to methods of warfare may do much to mitigate the avarice and atrocity of the conflict, but more than half the world know nothing of Christian ideals, and most of the other half regard them from policy more than from principle.

But the conflict seems inevitable, even necessary. It is one of God's ways of disciplining the race and teaching it wisdom. It gives himself greater authority in the affairs of nations and affords his truth an disputed. The Prince of Peace has come, but until earth is purged of evil and error his coming is to bring to the race not the peace of compromise, but the sword of conflict.

With the waking of the Walled Kingdom which has slept for forty centuries there is coming to its teeming millions of people the realization of their peril and their power. They see dangers that threaten to dismember their kingdom, destroy their ancient shrines, desecrate the tombs of their sacred ancestors, set at naught their age-long customs, controvert their forms of faith, and disregard their ways of worship. China does not yet know her latent power and her large resources, but when she is wholly awake to her situation and her strength she will be something more than a field of strife between foreign powers; she will resist all invasion with millions of arms.

But the eyes of the world are on the

of man has been fullest, and his progress greatest. Civilization has followed the truest faith in all ages. This idea of God answering to the fact of God makes the race optimistic and urges it onward to its goal.

The world is not growing worse. Mankind is not degenerating. The race has survived the fall of empires, centuries of bloodshed, ages of darkness, the extinction of nations, the doom of religions, tyranny over the masses, the throttle of freedom, and has risen to the sublime height of religious tolerance, political democracy, Christian enlightenment, industrial society, the advancement of science and the arts, equality of opportunity, co-operation in reforms, state schools and charities, free speech, and all nations have been brought into closer relations and sympathy by modern means of communication, travel, and commerce. Ever forward the divine Shekinah has led the race, and it has fol-

8

lowed with faith in its destiny. Men may doubt, but man believes. Men may despair, but man achieves. Men may face the past, but man looks into the future. Men may deny God, but man demands him as an explanation of the divine principle within him, and for the perfection of the kingdom of heaven in the earth.

CHAPTER VI.

The Goal of the Individual.

After all it is the individual rather than the race that suffers. It is the individual also that is conscious of life, that apprehends God, that anticipates a destiny. And yet there is a sense in which the race as a whole feels the force of any great fact. No blessing or calamity can come to any part of the world without the rest being affected by it to a greater or a less degree. The influence of truly great and good men is world-wide. Great inventions, great discoveries, and great achievements lift burdens from the backs of toiling millions who are grateful. Ideas that inspire, reforms that restore hope to the helpless, philanthropies that illustrate the feeling of God for men, sacrifice that follows the example

115

of the Cross, all touch the heart of the world as though the race had but a single soul. So also when any part of the world suffers from a great famine, a devastating tornado, a cruel war, an oppressive tyrant, a degrading religion, the whole of the world's heart is moved.

But the real sufferer is always the individual; and in his disciplining the race and his advancement of it in all that constitutes the world's redemption, God has sought the good of the individual man; the very being who has felt the keenness of sorrow, the despair of doubt, and the crushing burdens of life. And, though he may never have been aware of God's guardianship over him, though he may not have thought he had a soul, though the idea that he was appointed to a destiny divine and eternal may never have dawned upon his darkened mind, nevertheless he was God's child, and God was caring for him as a father cares for his own.